"*Our Father in the Year of the Wolf* is a book of beings and endings and beginnings. More particularly, it is a book about the inevitability of endings, which seem, in these poems, only slightly less fundamental than being itself, and the tenuous possibility of renewal, of beginning again, which only occasionally intersects with being. It is, in other words, a book about family. And it is beautiful. But its beauty is its own: These poems refuse the easy richness of lyrical language while retaining the rhythms of lyrics of high intensity, and so mark an end of one of the many family lines beginning with Hart Crane. In this way, there is no book like *Our Father in the Year of the Wolf*. It is, irreplaceably, itself."

—Shane McCrae

"The making of many books has no end, in one sense, because we must continually reimagine our histories: the stories, Harrity tells us, that "we tell back or let alone or live along or lift up high." His is an intense, complicated rendering. These mysterious lyrical narratives, lush and surprising, dramatize the corporeal manifestations of our most primal emotional and spiritual natures. How like us these formally inventive poems look on the page: broken, yet whole."

—Martha Serpas

"It takes all my strength to hang onto the wild ride of these verses. If not for the resilience of the speaker, the resourcefulness of the prosody, I might be at a loss. Harrity reckons with a father-wound so brutal that it has left him not only raving but vulnerable and exposed. When the honesty seems too much, the book turns unexpectedly liturgical. The muscular language of the earth and all its particulars—"horsewhip" and "amaranth," "melon baller" and "battery acid"—tells us this is a voice in the wilderness that must cry out. I am surprised at how beautiful he makes the sound of his yawp."

—L. S. Klatt

"Dave Harrity's *Our Father in the Year of the Wolf* is one of the most playful and profound books of poetry that I have come across in a long time. Its title includes the father and the wolf as iconic figures of transformation that play off of one another in a duality of the spirit—human and animal. Harrity pushes, thematically, a force, a gust of primal vision, through these poems with such a tender ferocity that one is hard pressed to put the book down while figuring out how to breathe. Harrity is a visionary poet in the spirit of Blake and Rilke and Sexton. He injects the English language with a dreamcatcher's colorful twine. That is, these poems play with language to get at the center of a psycho-spiritual reckoning. They are wickedly primordial, and that is what I love about them most. They have weight and body and funk, and they billow. When you read them you want to eat and scream, preen and sex. As the wolf, as the father, Harrity wants to "open your door and . . . kiss all your people." Eat them too, devour—as food and as celebration, a celebration of the human condition. These poems devour what is beautiful and dangerous in this living life. They are from the head and the heart of a man who is steeple and church, who is body and trope, who is father and who is wolf; and you should read them all, in a hammock, by the campfire under stars, and on the subway, at rush hour, where the throng of human stinks the best."

—Matthew Lippman

OUR FATHER IN THE YEAR OF THE WOLF

DAVE HARRITY

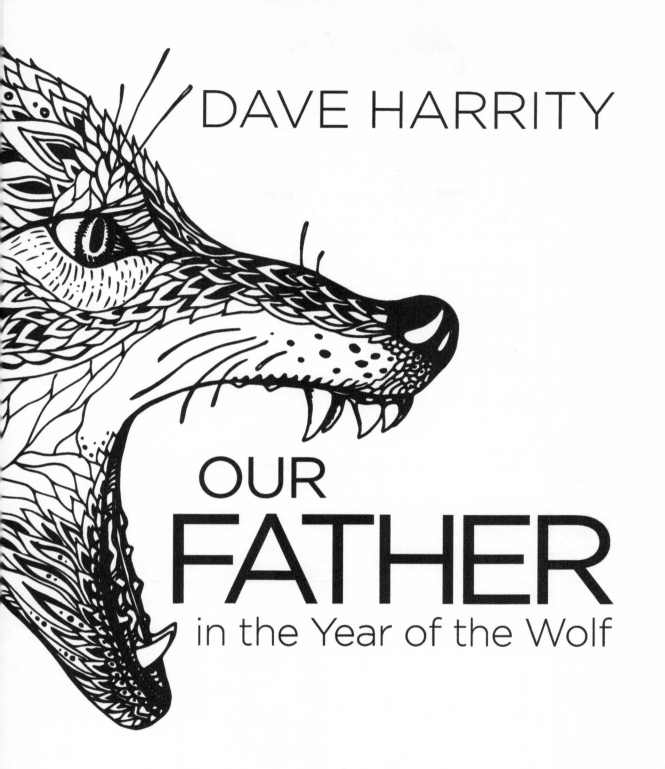

OUR
FATHER
in the Year of the Wolf

WordFarm
SEATTLE, WASHINGTON

WordFarm
334 Lakeside Ave S., #207
Seattle, WA 98144
www.wordfarm.net
info@wordfarm.net

Cover Image: iStockphoto
Cover Design: Andrew Craft

USA ISBN-13: 978-1-60226-016-0
USA ISBN-10: 1-60226-016-8
Printed in the United States of America
First Edition: 2016

Library of Congress Cataloging-in-Publication Data

Harrity, Dave.
[Poems. Selections]
Our father in the year of the wolf : poems / Dave Harrity. -- First edition.
*   pages cm*
ISBN 978-1-60226-016-0 (pbk.)
I. Title.
PS3608.A78385A6 2015
811'.6--dc23

2015035153

P 13 12 11 10 9 8 7 6 5 4 3 2 1
Y 26 25 24 23 22 21 20 19 18 17 16

CONTENTS

AUTHOR'S NOTES

General Note

This collection relies loosely on hagiography (the biographical narratives of saints) for some of its narrative and metaphor. Tales of mysticism and magical realism are common in this literary form of the early Christian church in which sin, martyrdom, prophecy and repentance are explored in compelling and often unorthodox ways. This book plays with the story of St. Natalis of Ireland, who cursed the unrepentant Altan Clan of County Meath. Every seven years, two men of the clan transform into werewolves as punishment for the sins of their fathers. The curse is eternal and fixed—an endless circus of lycanthropy damning the descendants to live out the arrogance, cruelty and violence of the generations before. Relatedly, some poems in this collection mention "sympathetic wounds." This term refers to a wound received during a state of lycanthropy that is still visible once the individual has returned to human form, thus leading the human identity of the monster to be revealed.

"Lemniscate"

A reductionist's definition would be an infinity symbol (∞), two loops meeting at a central point on a plane. The end phrase of this poem, *lupus est homo homini,* translates to "one man to another is a wolf."

"Her Snow Globe"

Inspired by an exhibition of the glass snow globes and photographs of Walter Martin and Paloma Muñoz, which can be seen in their book *Travelers* (Aperture, 2008).

"To David" Triptych

Numbers stations are short-wave, coded radio transmissions used by the military and clandestine agencies to communicate sensitive information, mission directives or, more simply, weather patterns. Transmissions on these frequencies are often strings of numbers or incoherent Morse code, repeated in unbroken circuit by a synthetic female or child voice.

"Our Father in the Year of the Wolf"

Riffs on language and style from Merton, Tennyson and Eliot. The poem is dedicated to Chris Allgeier.

On Composite Texts

Several pieces of this collection riff on a variety of original sources: The Book of Common Prayer (The Last Rites, Compline, The Confession of Sin, The Holy Eucharist and Collects from the Morning Prayer liturgy); The Book of Psalms (KJV & NIV); "The Sermon on the Mount" and The Gospel of Mark, along with other narratives and parables in the Old Testament or Synoptic Gospels concerning power struggle (Ruth and Boaz; Jesus, Judas, Pilate and Barabbas; Absalom and David; Jacob and the Angel; Moses and Pharaoh; as well as more metaphysical manifestations such as Legion or the Incarnation); "Taste and See" by James E. Moore; "Sympathy for the Devil" by The Rolling Stones; "I'm Trading in My Sorrows" by Jeremy Camp; "The Song of Los" by William Blake. Last, a variety of lines and sentence structures play on Robert Alter's translation of Qoheleth (also known as Ecclesiastes), especially verses in the first chapter: "All things are weary. A man cannot speak. The eye is not sated with seeing, nor the ear filled with hearing. That which was is that which will be, and that which was done is that which will be done."

ACKNOWLEDGMENTS

Many thanks to the following publications where these poems first appeared, often in earlier versions or with different titles:

Appalachian Heritage: "Eggshells Around His House" and "Mother's Crossword, #26 Down"

The Curator: "Not Simply Fashion Only Desires Design Over Functionality"

Floor Plan: "Declares Himself," "Lemniscate," "Threshing Floor," "Legion" and "The Only Time He Ever Cooked"

Killing the Buddha: "Nativity in Autumn Grays"

The Portland Review: fragments from "Equi-" (originally published as "Vapor")

Rabbit Catastrophe Review: "To David" Triptych

Rock & Sling: "Potter's Field," "& His Ministers," "Drift," "Moonflower," "Glissando" and fragments of "-Nox" (originally published as "Dissonance")

Revolution John: "Father in Middle Age, Just Before Nightfall," "Story Clipped by Mother From the Funny Papers" and "Litany of Aphorisms Learnt At Home"

Revolver: "If the Silver Could Be Given Back & Prophecies Erased" and "Second Law"

Ruminate Magazine: "Meadowland" and "Reverberation"

SAND (Berlin): "& What Is Done So Easily in the Left Is Left"

Softblow: "I Was Told There Would Be Cake" and "A Room of Father's Cellar"

St. Katherine Review: "Our Father in the Year of the Wolf" (published as "Theophonic")

Pieces of "Declares Himself" and "Care for the Widow &/or Orphan" were published in *Softblow* as "Dream Coming From the Head of a Staff" and "Dream of Why She Is Body Enough." The poem "Meadowland" was selected for inclusion in the 2015 *Orison Anthology.*

I'd like to thank the following editors, friends, collaborators, confidants and supporters who made suggestions on how to make this book better or helped otherwise with their words, affirmations and ears: Adam Day, Amy Munson, Brandon Waybright, Brett Foster, Cameron Lawrence, Chris McCurry, Claire Bateman, Jae Newman, Jeff Hipsher, Jen Woods, John James, Kirby Gann, Kristin George-Bagdanov, Luke Hankins, Lew Klatt, Martha Serpas, Matthew Lippman, Michael Estes, Nicholas Samaras, Paul Quenon, Phil Hall, Robin LaMer Rahija, Rod Dixon, Scott Cairns, Shane McCrae, Thom Caraway and Tom Hunley. Thanks especially to Marci Johnson and to Sally and Andrew Craft for their support and enthusiasm with this book. And, mostly, thanks to Amanda, Emmalynne and Gabriel, who live with me every day.

All rivers go to the sea, and the sea is not full.
  To the place that the rivers go, there they return to go.

. . . The eye is not sated with seeing, nor the ear filled with hearing.
                                                              —*Qoheleth*

LEMNISCATE

the month he disappeared I slit my chin shaving

   it was all white tile & red wine splat
small picks of thin hair & a bright-eyed scrap

   of cycloptic tissue shred that told me
I'd become a man & no matter all the times
   I did the deed or waxed whatever smooth

   the hair came back with each full moon
but father never mentioned how to keep it clean

just like he used to say: *lupus est homo homini*

SECOND LAW

Call it inertia, call it quanta, call it all-expanding star—ordered namings
of erosions or best chronologies of kings. Even as it's done, it's more undone in subtle backness:
cells degrade to cancer,

addiction leaves behind a small slug trail, eggs wither with the womb.
Tomorrow, the stable needs another hosing out & the farrier drives a flaring nail, kneeling
at the quarters. Outside, rain cuts paint a little more

or a screw comes loose & a shingle strides
into the gutter. Inside, the laundry pile grows as shirts give threads away. This string of simple let-downs:
what's bound unbounds; what's fixed

unfixes. & we follow one another forward from a rolling boil,
potential lives ladled from a pot of wax, then paraffin decorations, scratching pins. The insurrectionist
descends the marble stair free & clear

of treachery, so everything turns into easter. Windows
& doors open to the wolves we are & are becoming. One life strung out from another—morning din
rung mescaline—song not sung

so much as hummed, going on to be ignored. Moonlight
tinnitus & two bled shadows sheetless on a bed, haze inside the head like a secret middle name. Keep it:
dormancy of decay. Keep it: tree blasted leafless by the rain. Keep it:

half-red rind resting sloshed
white in the sun, a troop of ants away. Keep it: film falling from your eyes & devil in the chest. & what it
is & that it is: familiar sounds, parsed pitch

ringing backward / forward ringing through the dark.

EGGSHELLS AROUND HIS HOUSE

it wasn't so much his mess but the smell of it   waft of uncombed pelts

   dried with clots or gluts of meat caked on hooks   that dangled from the ceiling

garbage undiminished   in pooled wine & battery acid dandruff crust   a mealy stink

from the tub's clear liquid   & the milked fish flush of wet carpet rolled & moldered

     none of that compared to the disdain he held with silence   which we each noticed the most

common as a quiver of unfinished arrows or bowstrings slacked appetites   the stags

    & sawed horns of neglect   or the only thing near a smile would be the obtuse

elbow of a load-ready shotgun set out on the workbench   our never speaking on the killing

that he did but instead   our prayers for some triumphal entry like *o save us*

    from the things he did not say   *o save us from the coats laid down & branches cut*

o save us from the histories that we were told   angers that would flare & fade

kin to curses uttered ages back   so easily we'd cover up our shames

   these mongreled messes handed down   & promises unkept long before we came

IN THE PASTURE THAT PENNED HIS HORSES

A kind weanling, really, but father named him Gluestick & left him out most nights. I remember him best in the dusky gold dust billows. The little guy

loved lying in burnt grass or barreling bareback in soft clover clusters: a slight sweat in sun, a pulse vesseled in his neck, a purple scrim-light tussled on his ear.

POTTER'S FIELD

Across a sweep of grass, a horse is dying—wheezing bullet fragments strayed
into his jaw. Blood gloss swell in ivy-leek, blank-field snow now sizzled by clear sleet—a vitiligo
flushing out the green
                              of stories we tell back or let alone or live along
or lift up high. This field where we return to mourn, marked small with destinies we noose
around the neck. Here's the place
                              where we don't remember any names, where
we all stand up concussed inside a storm. A bullet splits across the head, a boy gets buried
underneath a branch:
                              exits & entrances nearly all the same, which makes an accident
a sacrifice you wouldn't choose to make. Doors become windows or windows, doors—
each decision made wishing clearer vapor,
                              some God-sent silver slug
to put us out to pasture—like beasts lie down & turn into their bones, like ropes run taut & swing
the family pride. What should be boxed
                              & buried turns to earthly pilgrimage, turns to
console the mourning, to the sweet disgust of sympathy we stitch inside, to the wink we give away
forgetting that we're flesh:
                              splinter's edge cleaving at the bed, cuticle bloom of blood
streaked across the nail—our bodies live in tiny hells like these. This snow keeps twisting
to the ground each year,
                              & this animal never lets you rest. Belligerent & beaten down
with nothing left to give but unnamed angers swallowed back: whimpered horse, broken tower,
indulgence to the king—
                              my God my God you say & yes & forgive me what I can't forget,
please sing it back to sleep again. & what can't be counted out is buried under circumstance,
what's not discerned we nostalgically divine—
                              lines chanted over bodies lurched in broken dirt.

HER SNOW GLOBE

Never knew why, but I always imagined the scene to be a Sunday.

Shaken, flakes cuneiform & bounce inside the clear lung of water. The characters of posed clay
staged in small-gulped tragedy:
                              a gelding's girth laid across a hollow log
beneath a bare branch, salt of earth plaqued in his limp yellow glower

& flashes of his skull cast out as seed across the blonded chaff. Then, jammed into the tree,
a puce sedan:
                    what was a woman's face behind the holed windshield,
her shoulder to the wheel, shards of glass dug in her sweater

& traces of her head splashed along the seat & dash. Shake & see
the goodness of the Lord. The sky coughs
                                        ricey clods, vermiculite—
swish to show a shirtless man an inch away, a pistol to his faceless head.

NOT SIMPLY FASHION ONLY DESIRES DESIGN OVER FUNCTIONALITY

So much for a burial dress. Instead, patchwork muslin—cynical sleep pajamaed,
stitched selvedge—as if in death one could be dressed enough.

Forget the clothes: weave twill & tatter of time itself, weave
thimbled notions measured & cut off. Little devils tightened in the gears

& the gods go on building watches, torqueing up the world—slight machines
wound up & counting back & counting back from center.

Sure, it's theological—ticked equation reckoning—but still there's beauty pieced
& tripping through the balanced act. Sure, that little sound of death

will pinch you down the neck, since who really could ignore such a nimble thing?—
nagging clicks & screeching coils loosening to spring.

IF THE SILVER COULD BE GIVEN BACK
& PROPHECIES ERASED

To wish it rewound instead of its roaring stampede toward significance—bellwether wonder
of obscure stars or cliffside holes:

                          take your place & like it. But this stuff—
what's said long before the event—matters little once you pin up some messiah, creating the event itself.

Old enough to know what's written down might come true, what's wailed in wilderness
comes knocking at the door

                          asking for honey or money or a warm place
to have a baby in the dead of desert census. & how you talk on such a thing seems silly,

if your side gets told for you, after money changes hands. Turns moths sheckled in a palm,
turns a tree-limb-human pendulum.

                      Never stopped to ask what it would make—fool enough to beg
the power brokers while temples turn out zealots to the street, mis-repeating everything you didn't say.

REVERBERATION

What seems like spring comes earlier this year—
cold limbo twisted in a nest. Near the field, a wren rustles out her babies to first flight—
such small evidence there is
of any sacred thing. Tied to seasons, we're the lonely thread
wrapped round God's imposing pinky, the bow reminding him that things don't make themselves.
Now, to the stand of birches
brushed along the field—bonewhite quiet gathering,
pink light hued against the vaulted gray. An unexpected spring snow collecting on the fireweed, & then
that quiet goes away:
pistol peals spit into the storm, cold lips blow
a bullet loose & a horse falls flat against the earth. But even that is easy to ignore when you
love the goldseal's simple swallowing
or the brimming buds of columbine & write the whole noise off
as hunting. Like hunting, yes, like hunting if you call a thing something that it's not & sing a lie
back to yourself. It's the shifting of the sky
& each of us taking turns learning how to wither, beatings
which we simply can't avoid. So try & call this to the front of you: the way it feels when struck against
the cheek—heat spike ironglaze, gall's ache
tongued & gummed. Even as they hang you up,
belief in what you cannot see might keep you breathing long enough to see another day. Sure, there
might be babies born to save us, born in sleepy towns strung
along the world, but that's hope's sickness
lush & bloomed—kudzu cramming phlox. So go about & fantasize the band around the moon
God's miracle hello, paraselene bracelet
billowed circle on a starry wrist, his whisper
through the knuckled branches kind, his hair an early meadow rue. The birds are trying hard to fly
before they hit the ground. The shot rings
its sanctus bell, its bruised apology. A horse
is bleeding out in grass. & you can't do a thing but lie down with yourself. & you—& you & yes you are
& all your walking to & from your evening doors,
searching hard for halos in accumulating snow.

TO DAVID [MORNING IN THE GARAGE WITH BONE SAW, CHAINS, YELLOW RUBBER GLOVES & HIS NUMBERS STATION]

                                                     . . . animal disease he passed
to me. Hard to know what was asked with the redactions. Aside from black bars, what's remembered
isn't just the iterations but the routines of his day—

                                              sometimes I couldn't blame
the angry phase, marking sanity's return by the purple spells of sky at dawn—
austere leavings, late arrivals. Less a fever than a trace of panic,

                                      like a faded bruise or newly noticed star,
restrained & distant & never in complete control. Sure, looking at the past can winch your balls
up in a vise, but not looking does just about the same—I understand allegiance

                                        kept him going back,
dominion jumbled in *which was & which is & which will be* & he'd wait till a moonbow clear & follow
what commands. Always careful first to smell for blood. Yes I know. Yes it is. Yes . . .

TO SAY IT LIKE YOU MEAN IT THE FIRST TIME

What is it confusing words you have with words
you're trying to remember
                                like what's the name to say when you're muffled drowsy
head-locked in an angel's elbow kicking, the one to say to stop the suffocation?

Some slow wrestle back from sleep & fingers
in your side: when you've had enough
                                & he keeps squeezing out your breath?

The name for him just tipping on your lips—
runs carnival behind your bruising eyes:
                                flicker mother / flicker father / flicker aunt / flicker _____

no remember what / who remember no

& all those other family members' branches Y-ing tangled into leaves

what's the name to say when you wanna quit?   What's the

MOTHER'S CROSSWORD, #26 DOWN

Like her fingernails, the pencil gnawed & short—
                a tic, her small specter of control. & this thing like letting go:
What's a four-letter word for "assertion or demonstration of power"?
                So few ways to see it otherwise when she's crying at the sink
with dishes piled up & faucet leaking or this, her armchair
                session to manage the slight inebriation. After piano, she'd rehash
our own domestic politic, shake her bauble sitting there, stare into the dark.
                Which is it? she says to me, *is it WARS or GODS or DADS?*
She was never great with riddles, always failed to parse the jumbled words
                & never played a mind game in her life. *VETO* was the word
I volunteered, but she wasn't really all that wrong I guess.

TO DAVID [AFTERNOON IN THE GARAGE WITH FEATHERED RODS, HIGH LAMP, EMPTY QUIVER & HIS NUMBERS STATION]

                                                    . . . I will. For lunch
a new blind code & no objective. An authority's neglect summed up in a machine-spat sequence
he couldn't quite discern. Cyphered strips

                               with messages instead of sandwiches together. By day,
he'd hide the fangs & nostril flares enough to kiss the poreclain-blushed republic's cheek & make it look
like love. Yes we should salute him for his service yes

                                   we should pin to him a medal
yes we should ticker-tape & grandstand & make parades yes a statue in the square yes he does deserve
a day in August. Yes & yes &

                        yes & all the things he'd done or didn't do
according to official records & whatever flesh of bulls or blood of goats—or whether any of it was just
or just was—rambles in strung circuit . . .

DECLARES HIMSELF

saying that what comes (if it comes at all)

                  comes in fragments   flesh naked stands

crossing in the mirror   barking out commands

              for razor & brush or singing poor-me songs

through mouth-corner hairsprouts or her concern

              for what the neighbors knew & yelling

he should come down off his cross

         so someone else could use the wood

but the devotion's clear

         frayed & steady knees of pilgrims with slack mouths

& oh-my-gods & sweet bee stings

          & ringing ears & ribboned backs

              so still the truth of it comes in dreamy slices

(if it comes at all) & if I could I'd simply draw a map for you

          penciled lines to where our coins

stay buried & all treasures locked away in jars

         & what I want to know that crumples up

in torn-away days or light twinkle-trapped

       inside a globe of glass to swirl

& white clouds silvered out above the sleepy barn

        or cracked & christened thunder croaks

or the bucket of hair he'd keep beside the washing tub

        & I want nothing more than saving us

simply from our bellies or be but / just not a thing

       except forgotten so why & why & why I can't can I?

& WHAT IS DONE SO EASILY IN THE LEFT IS LEFT

unknown to the right of the same body   all left hands
I am & can't pick up my friend
                          & on the day he was born early
he bounced up & came to & later did his best to walk

punch-drunk   plush   pile of placenta
but with years he became
                 my pet   my prince   foal of the same
fumbled family   his regal mane congealed in fetal skim

     I kissed him as he came forward

what I wanted was a mare but he was what I got
                     & from that day forward
he was mine-all-mine   hackamore or tack   it never mattered all that much to me

TO DAVID [NIGHT IN THE GARAGE WITH PLIERS, WIRES, A DEAD MOTOR & HIS NUMBERS STATION]

                                                             . . . to letting out the blood, a throbbing
virus that he couldn't kill. Instructions clear enough, but a source can't be determined. To make
an effort framing up conspiracy or fault—in counting,
                                              counting out droste mumbles
of his spiral winding in. Tell it as dashes or dots or as an anxious alphabet, it's tough to get past
his service to the noise. & the codes must have mentioned
                                         the beast that he'd become,
the gravel & garble & snow & signature & pattern that yellow-swelled his eyes. As swinging noose,
as starry field, as broken branch, as strung rope gnawed
                                        in tones to which he'd naked bow:
devil, butcher, bastard, monster. How to say who was the man?—man crumbling by moonlight,
his table set for guests that never quite arrive. This sickness, this . . .

HER: CODA

What resurrects a note once the wire snaps clean,
                sprung metallic clang thruttled in the air? Bestial groan
stonecropped in the hull, the dormant pinblock's bulge
                then afterglow. Her black eyes fresh & the snow globe
she kept on the lid prisming degrees of catatonia
                on the wooden floor. She became a brown-blushed key
gummed down, sobbing blood into her palms.
                A thud as the sound limps out the last—

& NOW THE SAME STORY, AS TOLD
IN TINY SLICES

isn't quite ambiguous but more puzzled perspective

          parsing out glittered lunacies

of wake or sleep so to journal & put it down

      & let the tally mark itself in sleepwalk rambles

that what it must be like to dream or eat

      or die or breathe are nearly one sameness

sung together no matter what the day or place

        & naming it precise becomes his voice again

malaprop or enthymeme & what rises

      from the past eventually gets called prophecy

becomes cast becomes crutch

       becomes hung up & cut down

& this is mine & this is what he gave to me

      son never knowing what the sin

never knowing small salvation

     nor sweet shenanigan

DRIFT

open windows & a haze of sleep to the hollow thrum of night traffic zagging
red-streak slits
& pearls strung out on lustrous thread

this trellis of rising vines to wind tangled
in a strip of dogwoods
white bloomed fishflower   all gates closing on the purple mare &

pulse lingered in the cheek   pillowed still enough   becomes
the heart opening & shutting in the ear
hammer landing taut wire over without effort to pattern torn back from the loop

we become wolves: skulked descendants   marauders gibbous
in the meat-stripped dusk   the heroes dead in
a brute-ringed aspirated meal

wound in small-dosed city light
beasts break open in the orchard leaves & fruit of poplars
muting silver of the moon so shadows

squeal of metal marrow & precise motions
wrecked in steel crush choral horns
snap & scatter   phased blank to a bleeding grin

MEN IN MASKS

Crowbars thrank the doors & hood. A man shoulders muffler & hitch,
another pries spark plugs from the sockets:

                        half-held smirk through the knitted hole.

Screeches the gasket cylinder drill: everyone knows you can strip a car down to its frame
& never understand that what you really want isn't made of metal.

& oil's viscous repetition imaging glossy stars. Can of gasoline, frame-skeleton hulking in the dark—
who needs the brightness of the moon when you have

                  an open book of matches.

FATHER IN MIDDLE AGE, JUST BEFORE NIGHTFALL

A cracking tire left in grass, the tufts curl out & cover
grizzled edges from the moseying goats about.

Who is he & that he is or isn't living anymore
with the sun downing on a distant line of ash trees,

the ringweed wreck of muscle in his nose & chin, veins
in the blue hour of his cheeks wrung water from a rag.

& HIS MINISTERS

A man knocks on the door, asks for shelter from the rain. He says
pleased to meet you. He says *won't you guess my name?* & what he says he says
without his clothes. What he says he says

                                       stallioned, swollen stone. *I'm the answer*
he says, & for now your treasure's tucked away, but you know exactly
how this has to end. Yes Lord please come in.

Point at nothing; save your precious animal—shoed & bundled back,
kept warm inside the stable,

                               even as an ice storm canters off the glade. Hard to track
the monster's movements in the hall: each evolution of his body

                                               tenored but ignored—
tail becomes body becomes head becomes tooth becomes your blindness
that the moon turns tide away from you.

He's taking off your rings, he's searching for the crown atop your head,
& clocks count out their noisy poison—big hands
knowing what the little hands do.

                                 Take a sip. Feel what I feel in my throat. More wine
he says. *I want a feast* he says. So you make a ham; your servants pour more drinks.
Yes Lord yes Lord. & everything you have is offered up to him.

The rain raps the wooden door, its gothic lust
for filling up the sea. He says *I am the church & you are the steeple.*
Words an unfurled prong,

                               heavy metal tanging up the well. *Open your doors*
& let me kiss all your people. & so you work to reinvent the devil
in a likeness you'd prefer. Yes Lord yes Lord yes yes Lord amen.

The seasons change, he grows into the routines of your day
& then it's winter:

                        can't find your coat, no face reflected in the window
as you look at falling snow & watch the butcher walking in—
lawn streaked in struggled prints & spattered faint with blood. Oh my Lord my Lord.

& he's changed the colors of the walls & bedded down
each woman in the house

                              & sucked off each advisor that you trust.
& now you're opening your cloak & asking for advice.
Since behind each bastard

                          is a bigger bastard waiting for the robe,
your friend keeps all your secrets, chestnut mane

& curling on his lips &

                  licking at his hands & moon is bounding silver
light across a scuffled remnant & bones are gone but you know
they've not been buried

                  & notice you're not wearing any clothes
& pointed ears & dirty fangs & tawny eyes
& bleeding paws &

                no no you aren't hungry anymore.

THAT ROOM OF FATHER'S CELLAR

Where the old mimeograph machine

                    (shaded by darkroom red light,
            the gagged man—clobbered, blind-
                    folded—with hands tied, with his
            beard braided, cock-eyed beam jut-
                    ting from nesting blackbirds, bent
            naked flipbooking the cackle of a horsewhip)

                                collected dust in the corner.

MOONFLOWER

                                                All night stems rise unseen & your dreams
running out in one storm from another; rain sounding off a ragged little horn, branches
wheeling round in fierce chill-stunted songs:
                                              how we're faint ink spilt from stars,
ashes likened into shapes, etching names in stone & hoping we become them—
green notches edging outward as you sleep:
                                          how clear-slacked lines meridian an aching
at your side, that razored piece once put down into earth. Don't you know
by now?—buried things eventually break through:
                                           how grief grows its own conceit—
lousy, crooked supremacy. We trim & trim away a creeping vine. Breath slow enough to be aware
its banded exaltations, möbius & close-eyed:
                                           buds bloomed bare & sickled in the night.

OUR FATHER IN THE YEAR OF THE WOLF

To become as plain as the host in everybody's hands
will always mean a subtle imposition. Humility aside, our tangled energy desires softer things: epsom,
balsa, albumen, caul

or an aria's elocution in the throat. Aware
the ash of autumn, strange variety of holler flowers, then solid states of snow—what ways
to separate ghost from bone or pain from nerve—

when is the essence saved
from the iron of the body? Like knotted hair balled out from a brush or fingernails
clipped down to the quick:

vanity in caring for a shell, bodies clarified
in sympathetic wounds. We cut, transform & cut again—made/remade

in histories of mutual sin.

✦ ✦ ✦

Always in becoming flesh the process cannot be discerned

cairn chipped & tumbling—revisions born
& born again till I ask what son am I & step forward into falling leaves. Till I ask what son I am
frail-heart walking with,

stirring up the curse. So begins what definition can be rendered
from the tattered family Bible, & what began in small surrenders dresses you in flannel shirts
or nightshade swallowings—

tomb of tendrils, hole below the branches of an oak.

✦ ✦ ✦

Each day a fragment of the story gets untold:

purple banner flecking stars, austere forest sprawl—
& it's her bare chest on the denim of his beard, color-flush in the lips. How something
came from nothing not quite the miracle

as attraction knitting them together
in itself. & fidelities they swallowed that made them stay & gather in the stable of my birth. & after
she heard angels sing & muddled litanies of psalms—

yet another savior born beneath
a roving star, dreamt magus from a foreign place. But no neighbors came to celebrate
another generation. A virgin only to conceits

& she was so afraid she couldn't help but walk away.

+ + +

Each of us a subtle imposition,
                                        each birth a chance to be forgotten: wheeze of amniotic mess
& blood for an entire night—hushed pile nabbing at the hay. A nativity I thought I understood,
just more human,
                        less to lose in theophany: meconium of a resting king. Or to be
a blighted man hung up, sulked uterus above a gathered mob—branch-bent pallor ragged
on the lip. Again, the thing I thought I understood:
                                                            golgathan clear & water from the side.
Me: kin to sins that shimmer dew. Me: kin to chores of tracing out a hand & marking heights
behind the pantry door. Each of us
                        a subtle imposition, each death a marching toward a darker womb.

+ + +

                                                What we build we start to worship—
tower, triptych, dungaree: the things you make will make you bleed, simple as a thorn
or skim of blood or uphill slog hauling a hulk of wood
                                        on which they'll hang you up. So slight
a miracle survival is when the gods you've made crumble with your father's sanity: bright veil
of new blood sketching in the shape of what was once a face—
                                        cheekbone slip, lacerated lip
& battered brow. Then you know it's almost finished: skin less defined than realized
to be there. Oppressor's rod
                                        broken on the calves, slip-spear in the side to sip
the honey down. Or maybe you'll just go ahead & hang yourself for seeing God. A wilted pelt,
a Son of Hell, not knowing what you do—
                                        tower, triptych, dungaree: what things
we make to rend our names to life & lives we live to live eternally
                                        & yet we're still afraid.

+ + +

                                        A science summing up all our cells or a chiromancer's guess
at heaven's guarded gate: how we know & what we can't. But carnality can't be taken back: weathered
cloth & punctured wrists, pangeaic tarsals soldered by a nail—
                                        sometimes I think we're nothing more than sockets
bruised & cradling the eyes. Plain to see the bones we are when hung above the earth, which makes it
time to ask a question & doubt the answers that emerge:
                                        what's throned in you deciding what is & isn't God?

40

✦ ✦ ✦

My god,
          my—god, yes—god the table set for guests who never stop arriving—god
the wafer placed on canyons of the palm—god the way I feel my bones pushing on the muscle—god the
way I keep the marrow in—god the way I then
                                                            forget again. There aren't memories
to answer for the blood patina on my teeth to copy & to copy

                    oh god skin of breaded life
                    oh god cupped in bled salvation

                                                            & to copy & to copy—
what elements I've dragged & eaten by the river under brightness of the moon. What—my god—
is done in one hand is left for dead
                              & never sees the sun again. I wonder what I'm saying
as I walk away, wishing off the wolf in me a less malicious grin. No ritual undoes
what's done,
          no ritual unshakes the devil's hand.

✦ ✦ ✦

An obscure leaning into absolution
                                                  with the body more & more a trope—
the curses of my fathers' mouths arranged like rows of pews, full silence of a country church,
or latinate grains of words I won't pronounce.
                              & yes I should be more afraid of what I can become.

✦ ✦ ✦

Here's where I can put my fingers in,
          the absence I can enter:
                              griefs rendered rosary to what I am becoming every night—
hungry transformation, field mowed in fall sunrise, lunacy like horse waste steaming in the grass—
this is how the body makes its mess—
                              by what it isn't, sacred circus shadowed, splintered
in array, rainbowed silhouettes of saints, knolls of crosses, fractal iconography—
& the gelding gets to munch again,
                              cutbank feast of greening tufts,
                                        needle in us each waiting for a thread.

        Does the skin diminish the clavicle's importance, to appear a shallow, rising hill?:
of course it can't—not one piece of me more lovely than another, but this becoming—
this *which is,* this *which will be:*

                              indefinite precision, shape
of what I am & as the spell occurs or rope swings creaking from the branch: what exactly
can I know unless I cut it open? Flex & blink

                       of autumn stars, vault pinning
high the moon. A moment in the wild blush of night when brightness calls me home,
into a cave or running blankness

                 of the pines—that what it means to animate
is what it means to be afraid. Escapes across the creek, breaking in to steal, to strip clean bones
of little sheep & try your best to not betray your kin—

                      what more is there to do with this?

Always what I know I know

               in flickered frames—dopplered movements unaccountable:
or comforted by light for sake of shadow—flurries edged & absent in the world, detritus
atoned, etched between

               the self & stars. A body wrapped in bands—
sackcloth incognito, tattered infant clothes. Flower lilt consuming tombs I never know I'm walking to
or coming from—always known by what I'm not

                   or want by what I am or wish
for what I cannot be: this line this line that I've become

                     raw-clipped elision & forcing it to fit.

                  & even in this curse we pass from cup to cup,
I still swallow up the wafer, stupid little moon. I still ask forgiveness for the man
I never really knew—his upright walking gray into the world,

                   the scraps of cloth become
a government upon the shoulders & a manger myrrhs the body into a shadow
of its greed. Kings send out their soldiers

                  & blood comes out as water—the faithful paint it
on their doors but still a generation disappears. & so it goes in circuit, power incomplete
until pronounced:

            father father where is it you've gone? father father blood against the wall.

-NOX

not the center orbited by stony satellite   not the dusky pull of gravity   not the wafer

of the waxing spell   not the glimmer out across the tide   you brandish newer clothes
parade a handsome fiction & kingdoms rise & kingdoms fall

      in phases of loss side-split with control
& yes my king it's all the rage in whatever country calls the trends & yes your kingdom

is without an end   little god-blind counting out & counting out & counting out this year
this year you've slipped off   slinked & stuffed

      into last season's brimming chest of clothes
twisted coat you are   can't you see what rises up to wear you? shroud you can't keep hidden long enough?

like before   along the boulevard   flared traffic & crowds almost mask the shred of bullets
then the woman holds pieces of your skull

      as one would a rind of fruit that's slipped
from hands to pavement   one red piece of the whole slumped   & cradled on the street

like before   to a mansion under turned-down brim of yellow sky   bloodlines bathed
with excess jewels   a man that you let in the gate

      will tell you that he's god & hold your hand
while you're lined against a wall in bled revolt   then devil-piled on the floor

like before to a desert mob   & you're the prefect bringing out the silent man-messiah dressed in rags
to say   part skeptic / part politico   your bit of disobedience:

BEHOLD THE MAN
& everyone looks up but no one understands what's happening as the hour's duty washes from your hands

all this to say the ending's never coming even as it's leading you along   that you
can carry a cross all the way up the hill

      & still not know whether you'll hang on it
then be lowered & undone by rich men from the flock who wrap you up & buy your tomb

how you loosen your grip   how power pecks the salt of you yes   how gnats hop face to face
how vinegar sears the throat

      how stallions storm each other's chests & hooves in tendon-tight
declaratives   primitive crave & cancer all at once

it's all the same you surely know by now   this back & forth & rise & fall   that fog & dew stretch out
in the world & fire glinting just beneath the skin

      that you can lie down in a wet meadow
& extinguish next to nothing   that you collect up all those stupid treasures & keep them in a box

that you're nothing more than sounds let out & ringing round some
needling   some stupid hums that
                                    rise & fall & rise & fall & you pull out your clothes & leave . . .

THRESHING FLOOR

                        Whip of him & drip of her: dewy crease
& parts of wheat for offering: endosperm, kernel, aleurone, bran—germs tangled
in her wool eventually
                    get washed away. To bake his bread—starch & batter,
leave & leaven—to swallow down the barm & let go pieces of herself he could never cultivate:
same bright smile of spring stable
                      or winter slaughter, clots scrambled through the barley,
ragged jelly thick-poured from her cup of life. An amaranth, an herb—reprimand inherited,
desire for a rule (ark & omen each,
                     & he's closer now to looking like the god
he thinks he is) the smell of blood does something strange to sovereignty: settlement ringed
through her septum,
                robe untied with silt & festered chaff, shrove & naked spread
over his feet. This gift, this gift she's hidden in her jar—mother of the living. This hex, this hex
he's pushed into her far—
                  father to the reddened dirt. How a rib's arithmetic
(equationed sums to measure out the store, to calculate another life as yours) becomes
dominion's stillborn demonstration:
                shuck & seed slipped across the vetch, insides
slung & scripted on the floor. She's crawling up his legs to take a drink. & there's no confusion here—
no tare between the whey & waste:
                   tangles, freckled thighs, shoulders
to the downing sun, pulsing where they've joined together, fell & pulled apart. & water is blood
& blood is water—oat-spangles smucked
                  on stony ground so to divide, divide;
subtract, subtract: math of heaven, math of earth. She spreads his cloak & bleeds above the ground,
inheritance scythed
             & laid aside—she gleans, bowing to a fallen stalk of wheat.

SOMETHING CLOSER TO ENNUI

balled black rubber whipped with semen
along a crooked cucumber's tight cellophane swell
beside a roll of duct tape

I WAS TOLD THERE WOULD BE CAKE

Such strange presents: first a crutch,
                              then an urn.
& she'd set the table like we were going to have a birthday party
with a paper crown & tooty horn,
                                        but odd things too:
red-eyed, voluptuous utensils precise on individual mats:
nylon rope, oblong vegetables, melon baller, nine-tailed cat.
It's heads or tails she says.

Clear to me that what's tied down is cared for, kempt—
an ordered alphabet. Who wouldn't
                              pass out from excitement
of stunts & safe words, woken sweat & sage?
What the musk returned to me—garlic ejaculate in beads,
                                        nocturnal fantasies.
& this course not so much a meal
                    as the promise made of one yet to arrive.
& it's all tricks like this
                    that have to do with the body,
not what I know the body to be—
                              suspended, sired, surged.

GLISSANDO

The feeling seems simple & common really, so don't pretend you
haven't felt it too—alert to every sting inside: ravenous to eat & claw & coo. To disappear
into a body like you might into a sleepless city—

train torrents braised candy in the loin,
tingled trolly bells—downscale whittled & unfolding swell, white-winged searching you by name. Skin
folds seeded empty—unnamed hungers,

lapping tongue. But power & how it's acted out
are very different things—inside us cities bustle, cities burn, & there's left a rubble heap,
so lust isn't quite the issue here:

the smolder seems to matter more. Take the barren blush
of country meadows, silence salted & restrained—the kind that lets you hear your thoughts
& wonder why you ever wanted

such a silly thing: smoky cottages nestled sleepy
in the frost of autumn towns, rusting chassis up on cinder blocks, blue-coal stupor
wishing for a better life—yes yes idyllic

country life. Here they tuck to bed pairs of different stories,
but not such different secret lives. It's all the same: stars throw down their leavened whispers,
snow curves down in crystal slips. & we know the end

as we know how it began: alone
& sounding out the fragments of our names, incests running reckless in our boredom—
every city, every town. Night to night vines rise

until you have a quaint square or countryside
& blossoms opening their evening eyes. Years of buried lovers, inclinations or desires; years growing
old to lose the pulse inside your thighs—

a tuning fork's hummed intuition coming to a rest.

LEGION

Not hard to see our principality when she's a moth pinned down to a board,
her posture spread to bent-winged charm—translucent paper held up to a light, withered-well
& beaten dry. Our animals find ways to exit from the skin:

                                          hemorrhagic heart, brain bleed—
maladies eaten in, manicured or bent. & it's said we can't control what can't be entered in:
a thousand names leaked into the vein,

                           pelvic incidental, haltered knuckle bitten down,
pinky pricked & hands around her neck. A wolf unknown inside you comes—chlymadic orchid
opening, matchsticks lit & broken

                         under thumbs. What must be fire—what must be fire
shoulder-pressed into the carpet—janus-skimming both her knees, passed into or phasing from—
the body has its ways of opening

                    or being opened up: a chicken split & stretched, as ready
for an oven; an apple cleaved to see its symmetry. *Tell me baby what's our name* we say & sows
stampede, a thousand lives

                  with each cast from the last, & added back again—each word
we swallow said back twice as fast, banished into pigs. Like we have a cavity or swollen tongue,
a cough we can't control—

                  pleased to meet you we say *tell me sweetie—what's our name?* we say
won't you guess our name? we say. & all the teeth we've grinned, & her bread we've chewed & changed,
& fist between her eyes,

               lung-buttoned yelp let to escape—snuffed candle, sweaty wick, dried wax
welted on our cheek. Diving from the ledge to squeal, wet-crunching down the gulch: a thousand
demons sluicing in her hive,

                      counted up & spasmed out. *My God my God my God*
we say. Her mucking out—yawning mouth, pistil push; purple pollen, flower pluck. Our name
in hamstrung contours—*yes Lord yes Lord yes yes Lord*—

                        strained & spit amens,
names wrenched on sheets, curtain torn & bridled in her mouth with nothing but the blood—
our names our names & thousands screeching

                    from the swine & living in the shadow of our stain.

CARE FOR THE WINDOW &/OR ORPHAN

Gal at the corner of the bar
a spent or bent cigarette. But the mascara streaked stalactite
really makes me
          want to pinch her cheeks.

Pleased to meet you. Don't I know your name? My my my beautiful
bone-swathed meal petite!
          What it is is bones
that make me itch—the knowing that they're holding up her back & breast—
welded column of command, two lusty ladders runged:
bones to bones!

Like she's mummy-wound in cloth
to be unrolled in one long swatch,
          an instinct flutter
leading to unstitch
          the eyes & mouth, less-suture all three other holes.

What I wouldn't give to be the beast
flesh-naked standing who wears her like a hood!

To be the mantle holding up her cup,
          the sinew licking clean & sucking up.
I'm blushed & dumb & shaken & convulsed,
picking clear incisors with a paw. No matter in the end,
all of me heaving small clay breaths,
little lobo I've become,
          twicethesonofhell—

LITANY OF APHORISMS LEARNT AT HOME

the body is small enough to be forgotten

the body isn't simple but precise

the body is a tiny atlas of its shadows

the body never tells you any lies

& love is more like disappearing

love is nothing like a name

love is notes of music never made

love is burnt so to be flecked away

EQUI-

. . . hooks & hangers bare inside the closet with the new season's warmer clothes splayed out on the bed
for winter's triumphal entry into town
                                        & so again   the world's subtle shift
to bareness   since for everything a season comes & for every river there is a waiting sea

we add in order to survive while nature strips itself to do the same   the trees go on living
surviving cold's stampede by giving up their leaves
                                                    it's the pith that matters most
pulp packed whole behind the bark   fanning out its hidden mark each year

it beats the cold & blooms its color back again   that's the instinct in the world
rippled loops recording life & living with the loss
                                                but we kill them
so that we can count the rings   the end so simple as it is   this world

where kingdoms rise & kingdoms fall   & you go about your little life while nature does its thing
building stores & letting down its leaves
                                        this clouding in the sky to gather up late water
yes yes   it's easier to name when you see it happening   lunar sequence

silvering a thicket's mown & unadorned obscurity or irises yawn to shrivel sour leaned against a fence
this is what you are & this is what it is
                                        each eclipse a small incision   room enough
to doubt a sympathetic wound   room enough to stick your fingers in

yes kingdoms rise & kingdoms fall & what you thought to be ascending
turns out to be a setting over time
                                        moon turning tide away from you with cramps of weeds
& crested waves riding out the their endless thirst for muck & sand & scree

how meaningless it is when kingdoms rise & kingdoms fall   & every day that passes
can never be remembered
                                    we're the ladder carried from the shed   & left to bead the rain
forsaken flaring nail still rusting in the barn   the rosary that's hung untouched beside the bed

the images you venerate shiver under dust   likenesses of gods   frail & final cameos
hung on any given wall that stands across an empire's sprawl
                                                        you yes you tear away & crumple every day
& hem worn garments whole again but still the bin fills & still the edges tatter over time

so you pretend a royalty & drape it round your shoulders   pack away your fading in a trunk
with other clothes

                    yes my Lord you look so handsome   yes you look just lovely in that coat
yes Lord yes Lord yes yes Lord amen   you're worth every word you spend to lift you up

& no my Lord you cannot see the seam & yes my Lord the thread is prime & no
my Lord the cut across the breast is fine
                              these things these things that you have left undone: & this is

NATIVITY IN AUTUMN GRAYS

Small stable & the willing body of evening's end:
It's brink & bone, a rabbit flashing in the grass.

Horses blur through weeds after an animal
that only might be real, tear after tear this season.

Maple & wind-stripped, slight cherried magnolias
webbed distal to glans. & once & once

he came forward from her into my hands,
his crown & ears & eyes sliding to begin:

that which is & that which is done & nothing new
but to myself. & before & before it was breath

let out inside her, faceless bundle waiting still:
quiet gathering I knew—& I & eye & I & ear

& this is me searching every year I've ever been
so to find a name enough for you.

TO ABSOLOM [FOR NAUGHT]

              . . . pulled you from the bundle of afterbirth,
as alien as you could be, emerging from a blood puddle like a bloom to bud, this unlike any other
surgery. Less machine than what I'd made before,
                & more muscle to keep me: medicine, masks, black bile
sputtering from the sides of your mouth. Small hand gathering itself around my thumb & helping me
realize what's obvious to all of us:
              the body isn't made of metal, not made to be dismantled. & it's not
a cervix but a womb—holy mechanism. & it's a cup, not a crotch—wooly constellation
wheezing softer stuff. It's these contours . . .

BEFORE PARTING WATER BEING PROMPTED FROM THE SHORE

Kissing my forehead she never said anything about the liquid or the mud

she knew I could become   & that I might become anything but

or else we'd both be nothing as the walls falling over languished fish

& I knew she'd drown   then & there I knew how I would end it

this of blood & this of water closer to becoming something I could never

STORY CLIPPED BY MOTHER FROM THE FUNNY PAPERS

That kept the dialogue bubbles inside & boxes for the bodies framed, so simply
she got used to saying nothing or let it progress & say too much at once.

What I'm thinking now is why I can't remember what it was or why
she left & then the voices found their way to me along the lines.

TO ABSOLOM [OF NONE]

                     . . . & veins of the temple door that stretched to let you go:
half-moon ear above a lipped horizon. & what it is is arms & filmy nails, obedience to laws you don't
know yet are there, or not yet there to know—allegiance

                              to the earth you'll hang above. What I had to do
so simple: scrimping what I could & selling it in chop, tried to raise you best I could. & once I dreamed
I was a king & cried the brambles of your tangled hair

                        & asked for no more enemies. But awake
it was the smell & gulp of you—little sack of salt—descended from the pocket of her belly, letting go a pulp
I couldn't love the way I wanted to . . .

THE ONLY TIME HE EVER COOKED

New nutrition for the two of us: chocolate candy,
bologna fried & sandwiched into crumby white bread.

These things are things that you have done & left with me
to do again. These slipped disc revelations, these

prolapsed ligaments. & what choice could she have had?—
muscles hammocked held me in & you afraid

to touch her. Every other week a phase, time when the moon
would nestle high over the barn its aureola dusk, radiant gray cold.

MEADOWLAND

Horse bones frosted on the flurried field—
rib cage crushed under a boot, marrowed hive of heat & sternum stilted to the ground,
matted clutch of hair. Body crossed,

body broken. What to bury: cranium, radius, tibia, carpus—
not crucified, but certainly a sacrifice. Beasts that eat the flesh but not the bone;
beasts shrined in cages

of their sympathetic wounds—tight-boxed curios or battered swirl
in galaxies, weathered sesamoids bound up, confused in day & night & sun & star. So easy
to get tangled up, bound into the field

of honeysuckle rolled chokeweed (lunged, released
& lunged again, becoming ghosts we don't actually believe) shadows ripped from seams,
loosed animals, beasts to steal away the blood

from the body. Beasts to steal away the body
from the bone. These little zoo mistakes in taking light for day & breath for life. So pick them up
& pack them in a paper bag,

so dig a hole to put them in the ground, but you're still
a ragged city labryinthed in a shell, swelled inside the sprawl you've built to lose yourself. You
thimble full of blood, you

jar of bottled air—taste & see you're still the sting & smell
& slighted skin—pocket bright with totems, fancies strung with relics that nourish not a thing. This
matter of the pulse you are, the pulse

raged in your prayers, idol counted out & catalogued:
vertebrate indulgence paid, silver coin patella spent—the purchase can't be counted out:
a colt's holed skull

gray & woven through the grass, orison said & saying over earth.

TO ABSOLOM [IN MOURNING]

                                        . . . or knew I should. Little son, I've given
to my greed. To never rise against, transform—dappled crux of what we were.
To reach you, cut you down, untangle—

                        walking morning frost, you'd let down your raveled curls
in the cold foal field. Now dangled there—purgatory, slipped spine. A grave reaching in the rise,
the sunken eyes, inherited vanity rolled back to my my

                                        my beautiful beautiful boy steaming
in the rising sun, away a night's whole measure: sweet & unknown god you won't become,
forgive me everything I've done. To turn it back to before, before when I . . .

BLESSED ARE THE PEACEMAKERS
& THE PIECES MADE

because once I shot a brown-eyed hare

who wandered through the yard

he didn't die but I left him there

ditched the gun & walked away

next thing is father

muscled crump & rusty pock

brings a flexing paper sack

flowered through the brown

as he hands me a gun & I never understood

how bodies fell in & out of

one another till I could hear

the gulping up of air

in whiskered grazes

this lop he passed to me

like his phlegm into the grass

like the bag kicks at my feet

its faint & sleepy

smell of blood

time to try again son

time to finish what you started

ABOUT THE AUTHOR

Dave Harrity travels the United States teaching workshops on contemplative living, imagination and poetry. He is the author of the craft manual *Making Manifest: On Faith, Creativity, and the Kingdom at Hand* (Seedbed, 2013) and another book of poetry, *These Intricacies* (Cascade Books, 2015). An assistant professor of English at Campbellsville University, and a recipient of the William Alexander II and Lisa Percy Fellowship at the Rivendell Writers' Colony, he lives in Louisville, Kentucky, with his wife and children.